Stingers and Fangs

Ways Animals Attack

Marilyn Woolley and Keith Pigdon

Revised USA Edition © 2003 Published by Scholastic Inc.
By arrangement with Reed International Books, Australia Pty Ltd.

Stingers and Fangs
0-439-64863-7

Text copyright © Marilyn Woolley and Keith Pigdon
Momentum Program © Reed International Books, Australia Pty Ltd., 2003

Every effort has been made to contact the owners of the photographs in this book. Where this has not been possible, we invite the owners of the copyright to notify the publisher.

A.N.T. Photo Library/Kelvin Aitken: pp. 17 (both), 18, 20, 21, 23; Pete Atkinson: p. 19; M. Cermak: p. 7, 9, 12; Brian Chudleigh: p. 25; J. Frazier: p. 4; Frithfoto: p. 10; Pavel German: p. 13; N.H.P.A.: cover, title page, 6, 8, 24; Otto Rogge: p. 15; Silvestris: p. 28; Klaus Uhlenhut: pp. 5, 26; Dave Watts: p. 27 (both); J. Weigel: p. 30; Norbert Wu: p. 14; Corel Photo Studio: image 427000, which is protected under the copyright laws of the U.S., Canada and elsewhere, used under license; International Photographic Library: p. 29; WWF/Udo Hirsch: p. 11; Simeonidis, D. Bios: p. 16.

Printed in China by QP International Ltd

10 9 8 7 6 5 4 3 2 1   04 05 06

Contents

Introduction   4

Snake Attack!   5

Dangerous Bites   9

Spiders Strike with Poison   12

Poisonous Creatures from the Sea   16

Using Poison for Protection   24

Glossary   31

Index   32

Introduction

fangs and the venom

The deadly funnel-web spider.

Animals can be dangerous or even deadly if they carry a poisonous liquid called venom in their bodies. They can use this venom to paralyze or kill other animals for food or to protect themselves from predators. Animals store their venom in different parts of their bodies and attack in different ways. They can use their fangs to bite, their tentacles to sting, or their spines to cut. When their victim is paralyzed, it cannot move or escape. It can then be easily killed, eaten, and digested.

Animals sometimes use their poison on humans. The effects can be extremely harmful and even fatal. As with other animals, human victims of poisonous animals suffer symptoms such as paralysis, cramps, great pain, and swelling, not to mention death.

Snake Attack!

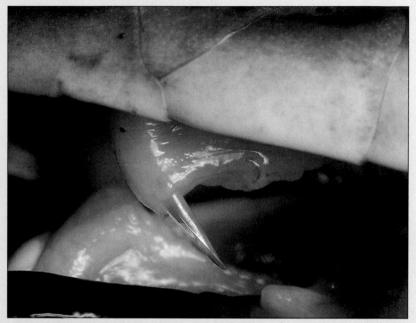

A close-up of a taipan snake's fangs.

Some of the world's snakes are venomous. Many varieties of these are found in Australia. Dangerous snakes store their venom in glands in different parts of their heads. When they attack, the venom moves through tubes to big grooved teeth, or fangs, in the mouth. The fangs can be at the front or the back of the snake's mouth. They are usually quite short, ranging in length from about a tenth to half an inch (3 to 12 millimeters). As soon as the snake bites its prey, a tube opens at the tip of the fang and the venom passes into the victim. Fortunately for the snake, if a fang breaks off or becomes worn out, a new one grows in its place!

The diamondback rattlesnake is the largest and most dangerous rattlesnake found in North and South America. It has a pit organ between its nostrils and eyes. This is a special heat-sensitive organ that helps it hunt for food. This organ allows the snake to detect warm-blooded prey in the dark. When it detects the prey, the diamondback rattlesnake rotates its jawbone so that its fangs are erect, and then it strikes. When the snake's mouth is closed, its fangs are folded back against the roof of its mouth. If a diamondback rattlesnake bites a human, it causes pain, blistering, and bleeding around the wound.

High-speed photography has captured this diamondback rattlesnake, which is about to strike. Its tail rattles as a warning.

The death adder with its prey.

Another poisonous snake is the common death adder. It too can rotate its upper jaw so that it is able to push its fangs well forward when it strikes. This means it can bite deeply into its victim. The death adder grows to about three feet (one meter) long and is found in most parts of Australia. During the day, it hides under fallen leaves and soft soil. At night it hunts for small mammals, birds, and other reptiles. When it sees its prey moving nearby, the death adder raises the tip of its tail toward its head. It then wiggles the tip of its tail to lure its prey closer. Once its prey is close enough, the snake uses its large fangs to attack and kill its victim.

A venomous coral snake has hollow fangs that are fixed in an erect position at the front of its mouth. It hunts for lizards at night, and during the day it shelters under rocks and logs. It uses its venom to paralyze its prey. Coral snakes live in the United States, Mexico, and Central and South America.

Snakes are not the only deadly reptiles that attack their victims with poison. The Gila monster in the southwestern United States and the beaded lizard in Mexico use venom to paralyze their prey. They store their venom in glands along the outer edge of their lower jaws. Using their big grooved teeth, they inject the venom into their prey. These lizards may bite humans in self-defense. If they do, the humans will suffer pain, weakness, and dizziness.

A Gila monster eating eggs.

Dangerous Bites

Another dangerous creature with fangs is the centipede. Not all centipedes are dangerous. The largest and most dangerous centipedes are found in tropical regions such as the East Indies. A centipede has fangs on its first pair of legs. It uses these fangs to seize and hold its prey. All centipedes eat insects, and the larger ones may even kill and eat small birds, lizards, snakes, and frogs. When a centipede bites a human, there is a burning pain. The bite also causes sickness and temporary paralysis.

A centipede seizing a cockroach with its fangs.

The scorpion also has a nasty venom. Scorpions are found in most parts of the world. A scorpion has a stinger on the last segment of its tail. There is a pair of venom glands on this stinger. This means that when the scorpion stings its prey, venom is injected into the wound. If a scorpion stings a human, the venom causes severe pain, paralysis, and convulsions.

A scorpion found in parts of Asia.

stinger

A European water shrew.

Shrews are one of the few mammals of the world that carry poison. However, not all species are known to be poisonous. Some shrews have venomous saliva. They use this to paralyze mice and other animals larger than themselves when they are hunting for food. When a shrew bites its prey, it injects its deadly venom through a groove formed by its lower front teeth. The short-tailed shrew of North America is a fierce, venomous predator that is three times more poisonous than the European water shrew. Its bite is not lethal to humans, but it can cause a long-lasting, burning pain.

Spiders Strike with Poison

A female funnel-web spider in aggressive pose.

Most spiders are poison-carrying creatures. They have a pair of fangs on their jaws that fill with venom from glands on the spider's head. Spiders use this venom to kill or paralyze their prey. On some spiders, the fangs close together like tweezers. On others, the fangs strike downward into the spider's prey. Spiders then suck the juices out of their victims and pass these juices into their stomach.

The funnel-web spider's fangs can only strike downward. As this spider attacks, it rears up, raising its head and body up in preparation for the downward bite. The funnel-web spider is found in North America, South America, and Australia. The Australian funnel-web is probably the world's deadliest spider. It burrows under rocks, wood, bricks, or the bark of tree trunks. It makes a silken nest inside its burrow with threads around the entrance. At night, the spider waits inside the entrance with its front legs on some of these threads so that it can feel when prey walks by. It then rushes out and attacks. The funnel-web has very large fangs, up to three tenths of an inch (seven millimeters) long. It uses these to pierce the skull or body of its prey. Big drops of venom can be seen on the ends of the fangs even before the spider strikes. People can die if bitten by a funnel-web spider.

An Australian funnel-web spider.

One of the most dangerous spiders in the United States is the brown recluse spider. It is also known as the fiddleback spider because of the dark violin-shaped mark on its back. If this spider bites a person, the bite begins to burn and itch. The area around the bite then changes color and this skin falls off.

Another spider with a vicious bite is the female of some species of widow spiders. These include the black widow spider and the red-back spider. These spiders are found in dark, dry places such as wood piles and stone walls.

A black widow spider waiting for its prey.

The female black widow is a much bigger spider than the male and is seen more often than the male. The male is often killed and eaten by the female after mating. The female is shiny black, often with red markings on her underside. She builds a large web with a tightly woven center. She preys on insects, puncturing her victim's body with her fangs, paralyzing it with venom, and sucking out the liquid from inside.

A red-back spider builds a snare out of silken cobwebs and traplines. It builds this just above the ground or around other places where insects, woodlice, and beetles walk. At night, the spider hangs upside down in this snare, waiting for its prey. It pounces as the prey becomes trapped. When humans are bitten by these spiders, the venom causes cramps in the chest, as well as in the stomach and muscles.

A red-back spider.

Poisonous Creatures from the Sea

Many poisonous creatures also live in seas throughout the world. Most people know that sharks can be lethal when they attack with their strong jaws and teeth. But did you know that sharks can also be poisonous? Some sharks have poison glands that cover the spines near their fins. These sharp spines can cut into the shark's victim and release venom that paralyzes the prey.

A spiny dog shark.

A stingray has a similar hunting weapon. It has a serrated (saw-toothed) spine on the upper surface of its tail. Poison is stored in the skin covering this spine. When a stingray lashes its tail, this spine cuts into the victim, and the venom paralyzes it. Stingrays can sometimes sting people wading in shallow water. Their poison causes pain and affects people's heartbeats, so in some cases it may cause death.

A banded stingray; (inset) venomous tail fins and spine of the spotted stingray.

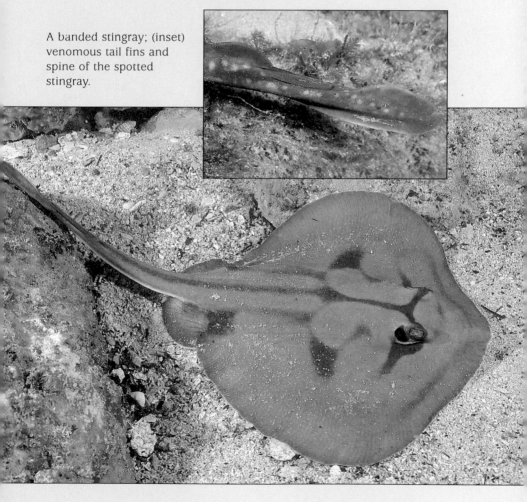

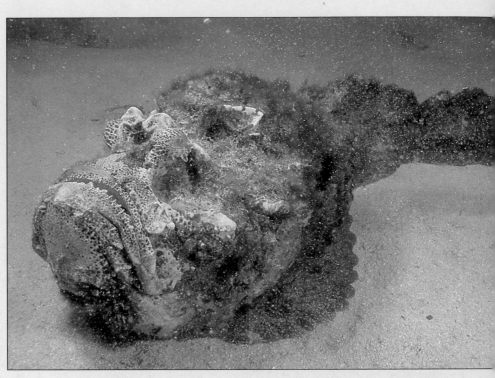

A stonefish.

Another spine-bearing sea creature is the stonefish. The stonefish has the largest venom gland of any fish. Its venom is dangerous to humans. It can cause severe pain or even death. The stonefish lives in muddy estuaries, bays, coral reefs, and tidal inlets around the coastline of Australia. It feeds venom into the spines along its back, then raises these spines and jabs them into its victim. These fish are dangerous to humans as their strong spines can go through rubber soles into people's feet.

The scorpion fish, a relative of the stonefish, is found in American coastal waters. It has similar venom spines, but is not as dangerous.

Weever fish also have skin-piercing spines. These fish are found in British and European waters. A weever fish injects venom into hollow spines on its body. These spines pierce the skin of the weever fish's victim, injecting it with venom. People are usually only wounded when they step on or accidentally handle a weever fish while it is buried in mud or sand. The sting causes great pain and swelling.

A cardinal scorpion fish with venomous spines.

Octopuses and squids are dangerous sea creatures. Many have different poisonous body parts. An octopus' or squid's mouth has parts that form a hornlike beak. They store venom in glands behind this mouthpiece. The Australian blue-ringed octopus is one dangerous species of octopus. It feeds on shellfish at night, using venom to paralyze its prey. The blue-ringed octopus sprays poisonous saliva over a crab or shellfish. It then uses its strong beak to crack the shell and eat the flesh inside. This octopus can also bite. Its hornlike beak can cut skin and inject venom into a wound. The venom of the blue-ringed octopus is dangerous to humans. It can cause numbness, paralysis, and, in some cases, death.

A blue-ringed octopus.

dart

A dangerous cone shell.

Cone shells are the most venomous sea snails. Most species live along coral reefs in the south Pacific Ocean. A cone shell stores its venom in a gland under its stomach. At night it feeds on small fish that it paralyzes with venom. It uses hollow teeth-like darts at the end of its snout to fire venom into the fish. The venom of cone shells is also dangerous to humans, as it causes muscle and heart failure.

Sea anemones, jellyfish, and coral polyps also fire venom into their prey through darts. They live in the seas of the world. These creatures have tentacles containing thousands of tiny darts trailing from their bodies. When the tentacles brush against prey, these creatures fire venom through the darts into their victims. The sea anemone, jellyfish, or coral polyp then draws the paralyzed prey into its body to digest it. Most sea anemones and coral polyps are not deadly to humans, but they can cause pain, burning rashes, and sickness.

A red sea anemone.

The Arctic jellyfish, found in the Atlantic Ocean, is one of the largest stinging jellyfish. Some jellyfish are more dangerous, though, and can kill a person with their sting. The Portuguese man-of-war and the sea wasp are some of the most dangerous jellyfish.

Another poisonous sea creature is the ribbon worm. Ribbon worms live in tidal areas around the world. Some ribbon worms are only a few inches (centimeters) long, but others may grow to nearly 100 feet (30 meters). A ribbon worm has a long tongue called a proboscis that it can extend. This proboscis has a venomous bristle that is used to paralyze prey.

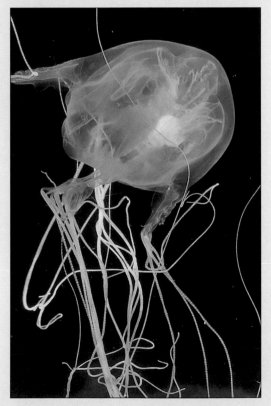

This box jellyfish has used its dangerous tentacles to capture the shrimp.

Using Poison for Protection

Animals can carry poison in their bodies to use as a way of protecting themselves. They use their poisonous chemicals to repulse their predators or scare them away. These poisons usually cause pain, sickness, or even death to predators. Some insects use poisons to repel their predators. Insects such as bombardier beetles spray poisonous chemicals to repel attackers. Others, such as the io moth caterpillar and the puss moth caterpillar, have poisons in their bristles when they are grubs.

A bombardier beetle.

The caterpillar of the wanderer butterfly feeding on poisonous milkweed.

Some other insects build up poisons in their bodies by feeding on poisonous plants. The larvae of the wanderer butterfly feed on milkweed and store the juices of this poisonous plant in their bodies. Birds and lizards that try to eat them find they have a very nasty taste.

Notice the milky poison on the glands of this cane toad.

Some amphibians such as frogs, toads, and salamanders also have special ways of protecting themselves with poisons. They are able to produce chemicals that are poisonous to other animals that eat them. The American toad produces chemicals that it deposits in its eggs so that other animals will not eat the eggs. Adult frogs produce chemicals in their skin glands to repel predators. The poisonous cane toad that has been introduced into Australia, Hawaii, Florida, and the Philippines from Central America also produces these poisons in its skin glands. Predators die when they eat this toad. Rough-skinned salamanders called newts use the same method of protecting themselves. North American species are more poisonous than the European species. The poison in their skin burns the eyes and mouth of predators. If they are eaten, some newts are also dangerous to humans.

The Australian platypus is a shy creature, but it too carries poison to protect itself. The platypus lives in fresh water. The male platypus has a hollow spur on the inner side of its lower hind leg near its webbed foot. These spurs are connected to a venom gland. The platypus will swipe at predators with a spur to repel them, or it will use its spurs to fight off other male platypuses.

A male platypus has a poison spur (inset) on its hind legs.

poison spur

Hedgehogs are found in Europe, Africa, and Asia. They protect themselves from danger with poisons, but they do not carry this poison around in their body or make it themselves. Instead, they use the poison from other animals such as toads to protect themselves. Before eating a toad, a hedgehog chews the secretions from the toad into a froth. It then licks and rubs this poisonous froth over its spines. The hedgehog can then jab these spines into attacking predators and poison them.

A European hedgehog.

The skunk is another animal that uses chemicals to repel predators. But rather than injecting poison into predators, a skunk sprays an offensive chemical when defending itself. A skunk instinctively raises its tail like a warning flag when it is startled. A pair of "musk glands" located under the skunk's tail produces a horrible smelling musk. Powerful muscles surround these glands. When the skunk is startled, these muscles squeeze the musk out of a pair of "retractable nipples." This spray can reach an enemy ten feet (three meters) away.

This method of spraying poison is also used by the poisonous spitting cobra. This snake sprays venom in order to repulse predators at a distance. These snakes are found in Africa, India, Myanmar, and Thailand. A poisonous spitting cobra has a flap of skin that raises up to become a hood on its neck behind its head. It spreads this hood out when it is disturbed and looks very fierce. It also has fangs at the front of its mouth. It sprays its venom from holes at the front of these fangs. The venom often gets into the eyes of the victim and paralyzes the victim.

A Mozambique spitting cobra in striking pose.

While some animals use their poison to repel attackers, others use it to kill for food. Whatever the reason, they use their poisonous weapons to survive.

Glossary

erect	standing straight up
estuaries	wide tidal mouths of rivers
fangs	long, sharp, hollow teeth through which venom is injected
gland	an organ or tissue in the body that produces a substance to be used elsewhere in the body or ejected from it
mammals	animals with a backbone that feed on their mother's milk when young
musk	a substance with a heavy and persistent smell produced by some animals
paralyze	to make another animal inactive and unable to move
pit organ	an organ beside the jaw of some snakes which senses infrared heat just like some burglar alarms and security lights do
proboscis	a long thin mouthpart or feeding organ of some insects
retractable	able to be drawn back in
saliva	liquid in an animal's mouth that helps digestion
species	a group of very closely related animals that can reproduce with each other
tentacles	slender arm-like body parts used for grasping and feeling

Index

banded stingray 17
beaded lizard 8
black widow spider 14, 15
blue-ringed octopus 20
bombardier beetles 24
box jellyfish 22
brown recluse spider 14
cane toad 26
cardinal scorpion fish 18
caterpillar 25
centipede/centipedes 9
cockroach 9
common death adder 7
coral reef 18, 21
coral snake 8
crab 20
death adder 7
diamondback rattlesnake 6
fangs 4, 5, 6, 7, 8, 9, 12,
    13, 30
fiddleback spider 14
frogs 9, 26
funnel-web spider 12, 13
Gila monster 8
gland/glands 5, 8, 10, 12,
    18, 20, 21, 24, 26, 27, 29
hedgehogs 28
jellyfish 22
lizards 8, 9
Mozambique spitting
    cobra 30
newts 26
octopus/octopuses 20
platypus 27

Portuguese man-of-war 22
puss moth caterpillar 24
rattlesnake 6
red-back spider 14, 15
ribbon worm 23
salamanders 26
scorpion 10
sea anemones 22
sea snails 21
sharks 16
shellfish 20
shrews 11
shrimp 22
skunk 29
snake/snakes 5, 6, 7, 8, 9,
    30
spider 12, 13, 14, 15
spine/spines 4, 16, 17, 18,
    19, 28
spitting cobra 30
spotted stingray 17
squids 20
stingray 17
stonefish 18
taipan 5
tentacles 4, 22
toad/toads 26, 28
venom 4, 5, 8, 10, 11, 12,
    13, 15, 16, 17, 18, 19, 20,
    21, 22, 23, 27, 30
wanderer butterfly 25
weever fish 19
widow spiders 14, 15